THE Duke of Edinburgh

Portrait of a great British institution

VICKY EDWARDS

THE
Duke
of Edinburgh

Portrait of a great British institution

VICKY EDWARDS

CONTENTS

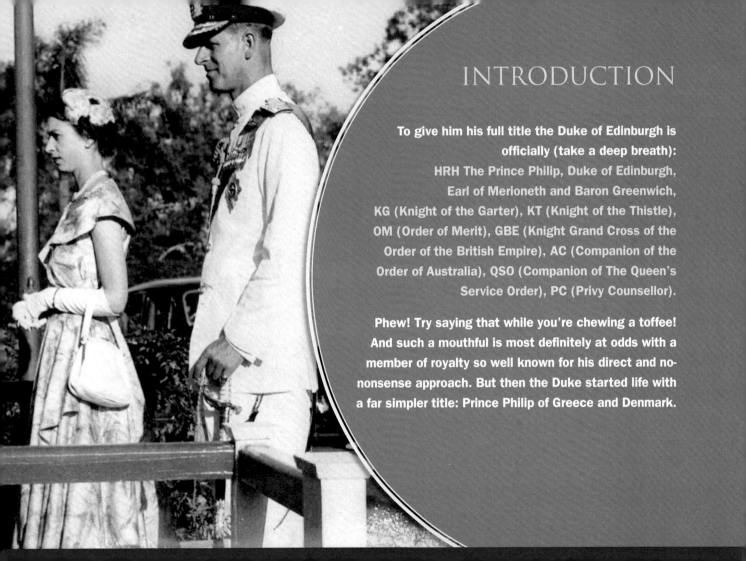

INTRODUCTION

To give him his full title the Duke of Edinburgh is officially (take a deep breath): HRH The Prince Philip, Duke of Edinburgh, Earl of Merioneth and Baron Greenwich, KG (Knight of the Garter), KT (Knight of the Thistle), OM (Order of Merit), GBE (Knight Grand Cross of the Order of the British Empire), AC (Companion of the Order of Australia), QSO (Companion of The Queen's Service Order), PC (Privy Counsellor).

Phew! Try saying that while you're chewing a toffee! And such a mouthful is most definitely at odds with a member of royalty so well known for his direct and no-nonsense approach. But then the Duke started life with a far simpler title: Prince Philip of Greece and Denmark.

The oldest-ever male member of the British Royal Family, as well as by far the longest-serving and oldest spouse of a reigning British monarch, after sixty-six years of marriage to the Queen (who calls him her 'constant strength and guide'), he is one of our most popular royals. Respected and admired all over the world, in one community in the South Seas he is even worshipped as a god!

And although his forthright manner has caused many a rumpus and often makes headlines, his support of the Queen, his quick wit, enormous energy and solid work ethic are just some of the reasons that he has achieved National Treasure status – an accolade that one suspects he treats with disdain!

From a rather wilful prep school pupil to an athletic Head Boy, respected by his peers for being un-snobbish and keen to have fun, Prince Philip's life, especially his difficult and unconventional formative years, could have seen him trying to garner sympathy. Instead his circumstances appear to have shaped a man for whom pragmatism, fortitude, stamina and loyalty are watchwords.

Most commonly known as HRH the Duke of Edinburgh, and addressed as either 'Your Royal Highness' or 'Sir', as well as many orders and decorations from both at home and abroad, the Duke also holds honorary appointments and rank in the Armed Services. Only the second ever person to bear the title 'the Duke of Edinburgh' as it has been created in the Peerage of the United Kingdom (his great-great-uncle, Prince Alfred Ernest Albert, fourth child and second son of Queen Victoria and Prince Albert was the first), the title will pass to Prince Edward on Prince Philip's death.

Now in his nineties, the Duke of Edinburgh's life offers a rich and fascinating history; from a successful naval career to his many charitable associations, his passions and, of course, his famous family.

A celebration of both the man and his many accomplishments, I hope that this book will offer a snapshot of a life that continues to be lived well and to the full.

Vicky Edwards

1

SHIPPING OUT & GROWING UP: THE EARLY YEARS

Prince Philip of Greece and Denmark made his entrance into the world in Corfu on 10 June 1921. The only son of Prince Andrew of Greece (the younger brother of King Constantine of Greece) and Princess Alice of Battenberg, he was also the little brother of four sisters: Princess Margarita, Princess Theodora, Princess Cécile and Princess Sophie. The new baby also had the honour of being the great-grandson of King Christian IX of Denmark (on his father's side). His mother was also of noble birth, being the eldest child of Prince Louis of Battenberg and sister of Earl Mountbatten of Burma.

Prince Andrew of Greece

Princess Alice of Battenberg

But being born into royalty didn't guarantee the young prince a peaceful beginning. The political rumblings in Greece at the time were far from a soothing lullaby and in 1922 his uncle, King of Greece Constantine I, was forced to abdicate the throne. By association Prince Philip's father was instantly a target. Sentenced to death by a revolutionary court, Prince Andrew didn't hang about. Thanks to the swift response of his cousin King George V of England, Andrew and his family left their beautiful family villa and, under cover of darkness, were evacuated to safety by HMS *Calypso*, a Royal Navy warship.

Oblivious to all the angst and drama, 18-month-old

Constantine I of Greece.

baby Philip was carried on board in a makeshift cot fashioned from an orange box. A rough crossing that saw the family stricken with seasickness was followed by a train journey from Brindisi to Paris. Evidently the future Duke of Edinburgh passed the time by licking the windows and crawling all over the train. The result, to his mother's dismay, was one extremely filthy infant – the Duke's natural curiosity was already much in evidence!

Settling in the St-Cloud district of Paris in a house belonging to his paternal uncle Prince George, Prince Philip began his education at a local private French school known as The Elms. By all accounts the young Prince was an energetic child whose school reports also credit him with being polite and sociable.

Wishing for his son to be educated in England, Prince Andrew settled on Cheam, a prep school attended by Philip's cousin David (later Marquess of Milford Haven and best man at the Duke's marriage to Princess Elizabeth). Enrolled into Cheam in 1928, academically Philip wasn't top-of-the-class material. At sport, however, he excelled. As well as honing his cricketing skills, he also won prizes for diving, hurdling and the high jump. He was, says his cousin Countess Mountbatten of Burma, "boisterous but great fun."

It was during his time at prep school that the Prince had to come to terms with his mother's breakdown. Whether the strain of her family's exile was the root cause of her distress is unknown, but by 1930 his parents were living separate lives and the beautiful Princess Alice was being treated by some of the most renowned physicians and psychologists of the day, including Sigmund Freud, at some of the best Swiss sanatoriums. Deaf from birth (but able to

Marquess of Milford Haven

Sigmund Freud

speak clearly and a proficient lip-reader), she remained in residential care until 1932. During this period Philip's older sisters all married, and with his father so often away from the family home in France – and in any case young Philip was mostly in England studying – it must have been an odd, somewhat rudderless time for nine-year-old Philip, who, closeted away at school in England, was at least spared the distress of seeing his mother's health deteriorate.

Although she did recover, in later years Princess Alice became somewhat nomadic. Once sufficiently improved and recuperated to leave hospital, and with her marriage clearly over, she eventually settled in Athens, where she chose to look after needy families of soldiers.

For all her neurological sensitivities, the Duke's mother was exceptionally brave. Providing refuge to a Jewish family when the Nazis in Athens were looking for Jews to persecute, not even when she was interrogated by the Gestapo did Princess Alice give the family away. With a lifelong deep and abiding faith, she later took holy orders, although this did nothing, apparently, to suppress her enjoyment of coffee and cigarettes, both of which she preferred as strong as possible!

Meanwhile, back at Cheam, aged twelve, Uncle George (Marquess of Milford Haven) and Philip's maternal grandmother the Dowager Duchess Victoria Milford Haven (to whom Prince Philip was devoted) gave the young Prince probably the greatest sense of security that he'd had since he was a tot (although the Duke has repeatedly pooh-poohed the idea that he might have felt abandoned or that he was in any way an unhappy child at this time).

As for his continued education, Philip was about to find himself uprooted again. His second sister, Theodora, had married Berthold, Margrave of Baden, a German aristocrat whose father had been Germany's last Imperial Chancellor. The educationalist

Princess Theodora

Kurt Hahn had been the Chancellor's personal secretary and in 1920 von Baden and Hahn founded a school together. Philip later joked that he was sent there because it was his brother-in-law's school - it was probably the cheapest way to have him educated. Philip started as a pupil of Salem School in the autumn of 1933. Hitler hadn't quite been in power a year, but nevertheless political tension was bubbling ominously and showing signs of boiling over.

A Jew, Hahn was arrested for protesting against the Nazis and fled to Britain just before Philip's arrival in Germany. In a demonstration of what can be achieved by

sheer force of character, just two years after leaving Germany Hahn had managed to arrange the financial backing needed to start a new school in Britain.

With the Hitler Youth movement spreading through Salem – the Nazis wanted the school to continue but under their rule – Prince Philip was

Prinz Maximilian von Baden and Princess Marie Louise with children,
including Berthold of Baden on left.

Gordonstoun was established in 1934 by Kurt Hahn

quickly shunted back to England and to Gordonstoun School in Morayshire. Which, if rumour is true, was no doubt for the best: the Nazi salute was the same gesture as boys at Salem had to use to request to go to the loo, which sent Philip into fits of laughter every time it was given. Had he remained, one can't help feeling that his sense of humour would have got him into extremely hot water.

But at Gordonstoun it was cold water that was the order of the day. Every day. A man with very definite ideas, Hahn wanted his pupils to confront their weaknesses. So it was that his young charges began their day at 7am with ice-cold showers, whatever the season and whatever the weather.

As one of Gordonstoun's first pupils, the young Prince was able to revel in his love of sport, enjoying sailing trips as well as field sports. Gordonstoun (motto *'Plus est en Vous'* - There is more in you (than you think) - was an outward - bound school, perfect for an energetic and outdoor-loving

teenager. Achieving Head Boy status, he also captained both the hockey and cricket teams.

But his character was already showing signs of being as straight and true as his aim with a bat. Known amongst his peers for being without airs and graces – evidently he never swanked about his royal status – he was also known as being what might politely be termed 'a bit of a handful', with a tendency to give cheek and general high spirits.

But his schooldays clearly left him with happy memories, despite the corporal punishments that were still meted out (and which he evidently incurred). And although Prince Charles later stated that his own schooldays at Gordonstoun were far from happy (and despite the Queen Mother's plea that Eton would be a more suitable school for a sensitive child like Charles), he and Princes Andrew and Edward also attended their father's old alma mater.

School holidays were spent with friends and family, mostly in the UK, but occasionally with his sisters and their husbands in Germany. He saw very little of his parents during his time at Gordonstoun. With his mother incarcerated in hospital, his father was by now living in the South of France with a mistress. If this upset Philip then he kept his feelings to himself, but it can't have been easy to have no proper family homestead to return to at the end of each term.

He saw his parents together just once more, but in tragic circumstances, at his sister Cécile's funeral. Travelling to London with her husband and their two young boys to attend a family wedding in November 1937, the plane they were travelling in crashed into a building in heavy fog just outside Ostend. All four were killed.

It was during his time at Gordonstoun that Prince Philip also suffered the loss of his Uncle George, who died suddenly at just forty-six years of age from cancer. For a young boy he had certainly had more than his fair share of sadness and loss.

Leaving Gordonstoun in 1939, Philip joined the Royal Navy as a Cadet. It was a perfect fit for him. He completed preliminary training at RNC Dartmouth, earning himself the King's Dirk and awarded the prize for being the best cadet of his entry along the way, in 1940 he joined the battleship HMS *Ramillies* in Colombo as a midshipman.

Six months in the Indian Ocean followed, before joining a battleship in Alexandria. It was aboard this vessel,

HMS Ramillies

HMS Valiant

HMS *Valiant*, that he played a crucial role in a WW2 naval battle. Just nineteen years of age at the time, the Duke's adventures in the Battle of Matapan are detailed in his handwritten midshipman's log book. Royal Navy warships were destroying Italian cruisers off the Greek coast and the Prince was on duty, picking out enemy ships on the night sea with the help of the ship's spotlight. Holding his nerve, and despite the enemy being in such close proximity that it came as a complete surprise to everyone, he did his job brilliantly. A career as a West End follow spot operator could have surely been a possible fallback plan had the Navy not worked out for him!

As *Valiant* prepared for and engaged in battle, the Duke wrote: 'The fleet's steaming east again and the future is still in the dark. Remembering the torpedo-howling attack which we witnessed on Crete, anti-aircraft action stations were closed up just before sunset… reconnaissance aircraft had found three Italian cruisers steaming eastwards in the neighbourhood of Crete… the enemy's shooting… was getting rather too accurate.'

His courage was recognised with the award of a military honour and, mentioned in dispatches, a place in naval history.

Promotion to sub-Lieutenant came quickly, after which he took several technical courses. From here he was assigned to a destroyer, HMS *Wallace*. Based at Rosyth, on the east coast of Scotland, he patrolled a stretch of water known as E-Boat Alley (because it was teeming with the nippy torpedo-bearing German crafts). The Prince was promoted again in July 1942, this time to sieutenant. In October of the same year his career received further acceleration when he was appointed First Lieutenant of HMS *Wallace*.

HMS Wallace

It was during his time aboard HMS *Wallace* that he saved his ship and its crew from a potentially fatal attack. Engaged in the Allied landings in Sicily, in July 1943, *Wallace* came under continuous attack by night bombers. Thinking on his feet, Philip instructed the launch of a wooden raft with smoke floats. Confusing the bombers into attacking the raft rather than the ship, which acted as a literal smoke screen, *Wallace* and her crew were able to make their escape.

Harry Hargreaves, who served with Price Philip aboard HMS *Wallace,* recalled the night, saying: 'Prince Philip saved our lives that night. I suppose there might have been a few survivors, but certainly the ship would have been sunk. He was always very courageous and resourceful and thought very quickly. You would say to yourself, "What the hell are we going to do now?" and Philip would come up with something.'

Not bad for a young man of just twenty-one, and certainly an unusually early age, by the Royal Navy's standards, to have accomplished so much.

His next adventure was to be a posting as First Lieutenant of the newly-built destroyer, HMS *Whelp.* Joining the 27th Destroyer Flotilla, HMS *Whelp* set sail for the Indian Ocean to join the British Pacific Fleet. Returning to England early in 1946, the Prince became engaged that winter – albeit unofficially – to Princess Elizabeth and his career progression continued apace.

After their marriage the Queen and Prince Philip lived for a time in Malta, where the Duke was serving in the Mediterranean Fleet and where, in 1950, he was promoted to lieutenant-commander and subsequently appointed in command of the Frigate HMS *Magpie*. Malta was probably the only period in their married life when the Duke and the Queen were able to live anything approaching an ordinary life. With her father still on the throne, the Princess was at this stage unencumbered by the life of duty that was yet to come. Shopping, dining out with friends, dances – the young couple were (almost) just like any other newlyweds, and the Queen was just like any other naval officer's wife. It must have been, with hindsight, a time of cherished freedom.

Achieving the dizzy heights of commander in 1952, Philip's naval career was to be cut short. The death of King George VI, his father-in-law, meant that life as a key member of 'The Firm' beckoned.

King George VI

But although Prince Philip gave up his active naval career ("my first duty was to serve the Queen as best I could"), his connection to the Royal Navy remained a close bond. Appointed Admiral of the Sea Cadet Corps, Colonel-in-Chief of the Army Cadet Force and Air Commodore-in-Chief of the Air Training Corps in 1952, in 1953 he was promoted to Admiral of the Fleet (he was also appointed Field Marshal and Marshal of the Royal Air Force and bears the title of Captain-General of the Royal Marines and is Colonel-in-Chief, or Colonel, of several British and overseas regiments).

On his war record, the Duke of Edinburgh is typically modest. On the occasion of being presented with the Freedom of the City of London in 1948, he said: 'In every kind of human activity there are those who lead and there are those who follow… I would like to accept the Freedom of this City, not only for myself, but for all those millions who followed during the Second World War. Our only distinction is that we did what we were told to do, to the very best of our ability, and kept on doing it.'

A significant event of his time in the Navy, although not connected with it as such, was his British naturalisation.

Although a Prince of Greece, this was only by dint of Greece being his birthplace. With his blood an exotic concoction of English, Russian, Danish and German, as his career progressed it was deemed sensible by Philip's uncle, Lord Louis 'Dickie' Mountbatten (who since Philip began his education in the UK had become something of a father figure to him), that the young cadet become a naturalised British subject, not least because he would have to renounce his Danish and Greek titles in order to take up British titles on his marriage to Princess Elizabeth. Taking the anglicised version of his mother's surname, in February of 1947 Price Philip of Greece became Lieutenant Philip Mountbatten, RN.

2 A ROYAL ROMANCE

Owing to the marriage of Prince Louis, the Duke's mother's father, to one of Queen Victoria's granddaughters, the Queen and Prince Philip are both great-great grandchildren (and third cousins) of the famously unamused Queen. They are also related through Prince Philip's paternal grandfather, King George I of Greece, the brother of Queen Alexandra. However, Princess Elizabeth and the young cadet first met properly when King George VI visited Dartmouth College in 1939 and Philip was assigned to entertain the two young princesses. Evidently a game of croquet was played and accounts suggest that the thirteen-year-old Princess Elizabeth was clearly smitten.

But according to 'Crawfie', the Queen's governess, it wasn't until after Christmas of 1943, when Prince Philip sat on the front row at the Windsor Castle pantomime, in which Princess Elizabeth was playing Aladdin, that the pair began to exchange regular correspondence.

King George VI and Queen Elizabeth

Post war, the news was greeted with much joy – the British needed something to celebrate. But not wanting to convey the wrong message (rationing was still in place and austerity remained very much the way of things) the couple were advised against a full-on pageantry affair and to keep the wedding low key and low cost. Or as low key and as low cost as a royal wedding possibly can be. According to David Kynaston's book *Austerity Britain, 1945-1951*, the King was warned that 'any banqueting and display at your daughter's wedding will be an insult to the British people at the present time… and we would consider that you would be well advised to order a very quiet wedding in keeping with the times.' So even though the guest list ran to some 2000 names, the nuptials were indeed in keeping with the times.

Although allegedly lukewarm at first to Philip as a prospective son-in-law, the King and Queen consented to the marriage and announced the engagement of Lieutenant Philip Mountbatten to Princess Elizabeth on July 9, 1947. Elizabeth's engagement ring was created from diamonds taken from a tiara belonging to Philip's mother, Princess Alice. Prince Philip also presented his bride with a bracelet, made from the same tiara, as a wedding present.

Sir Norman Hartnel

No wedding can be recounted without making mention of the wedding dress, and boy was Princess Elizabeth's dress something special! Designed by Norman Hartnell, the beautiful

creation is said to have been inspired by a Botticelli painting. Made from duchesse satin, with motifs of star lilies and orange blossoms, Princess Elizabeth had to use ration coupons to purchase the material, which given that the frock had a 13ft long train attached to it, must have taken a fair few coupons.

Apparently nervous but chipper on the morning of his marriage, which took place on 20 November 1947 at Westminster Abbey, the bridegroom slipped into the Abbey quietly by the Poets' Corner door to wait nervously for his

bride. Meanwhile Princess Elizabeth was just recovering her composure following a last-minute panic. She wanted to wear the pearls her parents had given her as a wedding present, but at the last minute they went missing. They were soon discovered to be half a mile away at St James's Palace, and a member of staff was tasked with scooting through the crowds to retrieve them.

Pearls in place, the bride arrived and the ceremony began. The hymns were *Praise my Soul, the King of Heaven* and *The Lord's my Shepherd*. The couple's exit music was Mendelssohn's *Wedding March*. The Dean of Westminster, Dr Alan Don, read the opening sentences of the service according to the 1662 Book of Common Prayer, and the Archbishop of Canterbury, Dr Geoffrey Fisher, by permission of the Dean, conducted the remainder of the ceremony. By all accounts it was a wonderful service, rich in solemnity but also glamorous – the young couple made an extremely striking pair.

The King gave permission for the procession to be filmed, with only still photography permitted during the service. Radio journalists had no choice but to to squeeze into the organ loft with the choir.

The couple went to Buckingham Palace after the ceremony where, to the crowd's delight, they waved from the balcony.

The day after the wedding Princess Elizabeth followed a royal tradition started by her mother of sending her wedding bouquet back to the Abbey to be laid on the grave of the Unknown Warrior.

As for gifts, more than 2,500 wedding presents arrived from around the world. These were displayed at St James's Palace, where the royal couple no doubt took their time in examining them. The 10,000 telegrams of congratulations must have taken a while to read, too.

For the newly-created Duke of Edinburgh (Philip was created Duke of Edinburgh, Earl of Merioneth and Baron Greenwich with the style of His Royal Highness and appointed a Knight of the Garter by the King just prior to the wedding; ten years later the Queen accorded him the style and title of a Prince of the United Kingdom) it was to be the first time that he had really been in the spotlight and the subject of such public scrutiny. The marriage saw some 200 million listeners worldwide turning on their wirelesses to hear the ceremony and people said that it was so moving that they could visualise the whole thing in their heads. A huge contrast to the high definition big-screen viewing of the more modern-day recent royal weddings.

The honeymoon began as the couple, joined by the Princess's beloved corgi, Susan, boarded a train at Waterloo Station. The wedding night was spent at Broadlands, home to Philip's uncle, the Earl of Mountbatten. From here the newlyweds headed for Birkhall on the Balmoral Estate.

The first of the couple's children, Prince Charles, was born in 1948. Anne followed in 1950. But by the time Prince Andrew and Prince Edward came along, their parents were running the royal show.

Queen Mary

In February 1952, King George VI died and Elizabeth, his eldest daughter, became Queen. But what should the new 'house' be called? Queen Mary and Winston Churchill were insistent that the next generation of the monarchy should continue as the House of Windsor rather than taking on Mountbatten, Philip's surname, as this was a surname that he had adopted when he had been naturalised and had no 'roots'. It is reported that the Duke felt that this was wrong and that he suggested that 'The House of Edinburgh' would be an appropriate compromise of styling. However, even though he complained that he was the only man in England who wasn't allowed to give his name to his children, Queen Mary and Mr Churchill had got their way. By 1960 when Prince Andrew was born, with Prince Edward completing the family four years later, the House of Windsor was firmly established.

(According to the website royal.gov.uk members of the Royal Family who are entitled to the style and dignity of HRH Prince or Princess do not need a surname, but if at any time any of them do need a surname (such as upon marriage), that surname is Mountbatten-Windsor.)

Husband and Consort

"Where did you get that hat?"
The Duke of Edinburgh to the Queen on
her Coronation, 1953

At the Queen's Coronation the Duke was required to make a pledge. Kneeling before the Queen and placing his hands between hers he said: 'I Philip, Duke of Edinburgh, do

Queen Elizabeth II and Prince Philip, Duke of Edinburgh. Coronation portrait, June 1953, London, England. Credit: Library and Archives Canada/K-0000047

1953 coronation ticket

become your liege man of life and limb, and of earthly worship; and faith and truth will I bear unto you, to live and die, against all manner of folks. So help me God.' Moments later his wife became Her Most Excellent Majesty Elizabeth the Second, by the Grace of God of the United Kingdom of Great Britain and Northern Ireland and of her Other Realms and Territories Queen, Head of the Commonwealth, Defender of the Faith.

And nobody can say that he hasn't kept his word. Whatever ups and downs the Royal Family may have had, the Queen's husband has always been rock-steady as her Consort. The Duke's friend and former employee Mike Parker once said of the Duke's devotion to the Queen: 'He told me the first day he offered me my job that his job, first, second and last, was never to let her down.' Which considering that there were senior courtiers at the time who were extremely sniffy – rude even – about whether the Prince was good enough to marry the Princess Elizabeth, is almost amusing. It's certainly a big 'in your face!' to the snobby doubters.

Since his marriage to the Queen, the Duke of Edinburgh has always played a significant part in national life. Accompanying the Queen on all her Commonwealth

Photograph of the Royal Family in attendance at the coronation of Queen Elizabeth II

Coronation of Queen Elizabeth II

tours and state visits overseas, as well as on the numerous visits right across the United Kingdom, he has been a loyal and loving husband, supporting her every step of whichever way her schedule dictates.

But what does the Duke of Edinburgh actually do; what is the job description for the man married to the monarch? In an interview with the BBC, the Duke said that he had to carve out his role as the Queen's Consort "by trial and error". "There was no precedent. If I asked somebody, 'What do you expect me to do?' they all looked blank. They had no idea, nobody had much idea." Typically, and to coin one of his own oft-used phrases, the Duke just got on with it. And so, in addition to supporting the Queen in all her public duties, the Duke also has his own schedule, which given the extent of his involvement with charities and organisations amounts to a diary that is almost always chock-full of events, engagements and meetings. Until recently he carried out approximately 350 engagements every year – staggering by anyone's standards, but especially so when you consider his advanced age.

Accompanying the Queen on almost all of her official visits, Prince Philip also has a bulging postbag to contend

Greeting Prince Philip, Duke of Edinburgh, during the royal visit in 1954

with. Letters from members of the public, organisations inviting him to visit, unveil plaques, make speeches or to write a few words of encouragement or endorsement – on top of all these calls on his time there are, of course, the official requests from the royal press office. And that's before you factor in his involvement in the running of the royal estates.

But quite apart from the workload, it can't be easy being the wing man of the most famous woman in the country. After his wife was crowned Queen, their relative privacy, and with it any remote chance of a normal life with their young family, went out of the window. Knowing that from the moment she ascended the throne he would always find himself two steps behind his wife in public life must have been, at best, an odd position for natural leader Philip to be in. But nevertheless his staunch support has always been absolute and unequivocal. In private, however, their partnership continued as it always had; with the Duke firmly head of his family.

Their friends and close family have always insisted that their marriage is as full of warmth and humour as it is of the same spats that couples everywhere have. One such account tells of a car journey when the Duke was driving and the Queen was his passenger. With his foot rather closer to the floor than Her Majesty found comfortable, she asked him to slow down. The response was one that almost all women who have ever urged the same caution will be familiar with: "One more peep out of you and you can walk the rest of the way!" As he continued resolutely at the same speed, one imagines that the rest of the journey was completed in a somewhat icy silence!

What must be both difficult to comprehend and extremely distressing for this devoted couple is the failure of their children's marriages. Only Edward has (thus far) managed to make a happy first marriage, with Andrew still alone following his divorce from Sarah Ferguson. The period during which Charles and Diana were so publicly scrapping and point-scoring with one another must have been an especially puzzling and mortifying time for the older couple, for whom washing one's royal laundry in public – through the press in many cases – must have been as shocking as it was cause for anxiety.

According to a report, one of the Queen's ladies-in-waiting claimed. "This was easily the worst period of their

The Earl and Countess of Wessex - 2010

marriage. They couldn't really understand what was going wrong when their own marriage was so good."

the Duke and Duchess of York on their wedding day.

But while their own marriage has endured, is the partnership between the Queen and the Duke still a love match – those closest to them at the time of their wedding are adamant that they certainly were very much in love – or has it, over time, become a bond that is based more on a sense of duty? Those who have observed the couple at close quarters over the years are adamant: they adore each other. They are also great friends and allies.

They say that opposites attract and Philip and Elizabeth are, by all accounts, very different personalities. The Queen is said to be naturally very measured and placid, a thinker and a planner rather than given to spontaneity. But then spontaneity isn't really an appropriate character trait for a reigning monarch, so perhaps this has been cultivated through necessity. Either way, the Duke by contrast is more likely to speak as he finds (sometimes with repercussions) and is more intellectual and more gregarious than his wife. Factoring in their characters and dispositions, their very different upbringings and of course the pressures that being arguably the most famous couple in the world places on them, maintaining a happy marriage must have had its challenges over the years. But whether their differences create the perfect balance, or they have had to work like stink to keep the good ship matrimony afloat, there is a deep and abiding affection between the two.

Unsurprisingly, there have been rumours over the years. As a young man Philip was gorgeous – the ultimate Fine Young Man in Uniform. And although claims that he had scores of girlfriends prior to marriage were rubbished by his long-term friend Mike Parker ("we were young, we had

Queen Elizabeth II and Prince Philip, Duke of Edinburgh, arrive at Government House, Brisbane during their visit to Queensland in March 1954.

Queen Elizabeth II and Prince Philip en route to Eagle Farm Airport, Brisbane, Queensland, 1954. The Queen and Prince Philip waved to Brisbane crowds on the way to Eagle Farm Airport where they were due to leave for Townsville on Friday 12 March 1954.

"incandescent. He was very, very angry. And deeply hurt." And given that the general rule of thumb is that royalty never speak out on such matters, it is surely a measure of the Queen's outrage and upset that she made an official and absolute denial: "It is quite untrue that there is any rift between the Queen and the Duke."

The Royal Yacht Britannia

fun, we had a few drinks, we might have gone dancing, but that was it"), there have been mutterings about indiscretions over the years. And with duty demanding that they are often forced to lead separate lives, speculation and tittle-tattle must have become a wearisome inevitably. In one instance in the late 1950s the Duke, according to Mike Parker, was:

So what was the trigger for such speculation? In 1956 the Duke took the Royal Yacht HMY *Britannia* on a lengthy cruise. Kicking off with the acceptance of an invitation to open the Olympic Games in Melbourne, a

tour of parts of the Commonwealth and the Empire followed, and he was away from his family for some four months. Suggesting that it was the marriage as well as *Britannia* that was in deep water, press reports were snide and without any foundation. The simple explanation, that he was taking the royal yacht to parts of the Commonwealth that had hitherto never been visited by a senior royal before, was brushed aside in favour of juicy gossip. Unusual as it is for the Royal Family to defend their position or to explain themselves, on this occasion the Queen did just that, using her Christmas message to make the point. "If my husband cannot be at home on Christmas Day I could not wish for a better reason than that he is travelling to other parts of the Commonwealth and that he has been to places that I have never seen". In other words, put that in your pipe and smoke it!

Without even thinking about the practicalities – for someone who has spent most of his married life with at least one detective permanently in his shadow, shenanigans of the extra-marital variety would be exceedingly tricky to achieve – aspersions have still been cast. But those closest to them have gone on the record to rubbish any suggestions of affairs, maintaining that the couple are actually far closer than their public personas suggest. They are, according to the most reliable sources, a couple who have always been and continue to be, devoted to one another; deeply respectful of one another and yes, very much in love. Friends of the Duke have, over the years, revealed that in private his affection for his wife is obvious. "After sixty years what is so lovely is that they are still so much in love with each other," said Lady Pamela Hicks, the Duke's cousin. Likewise, it was clear to the world that the Queen still adores her man when, in her speech in 1997 on the occasion of their golden wedding anniversary she said: "He is someone who doesn't take easily to compliments. He has, quite simply, been my strength and stay all these years, and I, and his whole family, and this and many other countries, owe him a debt greater than he would ever claim or we shall ever know."

Royal biographer Hugo Vickers observes that the Duke is the only person who can say whatever he likes to the Queen, "and I'm in no doubt that he does". Which for a woman surrounded by so much bowing and scraping must be blissfully refreshing and reassuring – she knows that he will be honest with her, because he loves her.

3 PERSONALITY & PASSIONS

Much has been written about the man behind the title. Often accused of being direct – rude, even – the Duke of Edinburgh gets more than his fair share of flak. But researching the opinions of those who have encountered him on a personal level reveals a man to whom there is a great deal more than meets the eye.

Royal biographer Gyles Brandreth describes him as being protective of his privacy, not given to wearing his heart on his sleeve, perverse, visionary, kindly and caring. Another royal biographer, Tim Heald, says that he is complex; inconsistent, exasperating, quixotic and mercurial. Other accounts present him as a man without self-interest but naturally curious about others. Integrity, loyalty, tetchiness, self-sufficiency, stubbornness, stoicism and funny are also words that crop up repeatedly when trying to get a sense of the Duke's personality. When you add all of these interpretations together the result is something of a conundrum. Perhaps he is all of these things to a greater or lesser degree, but as the Duke is reticent when it comes to talking about himself we shall perhaps never really be able to do more than guess at his character in anything more than a general way.

But kindness and humour are traits that are often mentioned in connection with the Duke. Broadcast journalist Pete Denton met him at a royal garden party at Buckingham Palace and tells the following story, which

> "My father plain and simply is very modest about himself and doesn't believe in talking about himself"
>
> *Prince Edward, Earl of Wessex*

encapsulates the Duke's tendency to want to put people at their ease in his company as well as his sometimes direct but relaxed wit:

To be honest, I was only there because my Dad's invitation

permitted two close family members to attend and, being an only child, that pretty much secured a free pass for me and Mum. After

> "He's formidable, he's daunting, partly because of his position, but also because he is a very considerable intellect"
>
> *David Attenborough*

going over the necessary protocol with Palace officials, I was fully prepared for my 'handshake, bow and smile' experience. Despite being 21 and trying to play it cool, I can still distinctly remember the hairs going up on the back of my neck as the Queen and her husband paused at the top of a suitably regal-looking stone staircase for the National Anthem. They then made their way into the grounds to meet the plebs. Being the youngest (but not the shortest) member of the Denton clan, I was greeted last by Prince Philip. I remember he said 'Hello' and offered his hand. I shook it, did a head bow and replied with 'Your Highness' as per the instructions. He then asked me what I did and when I told him I was studying at Exeter University it prompted great guffaws. His grandson, Peter, had not long finished his degree in Sports Science there. We had a *quick chat about rugby before HRH asked what subject I was studying. When I told him 'Sociology' he threw his head back with laughter and cried 'What the bloody hell are you studying that for?!' The honest answer was that I blindly picked a course that wouldn't require me to re-sit any A-levels, but I resorted to a more diplomatic shrug of the shoulders and genuine chuckle. He wished me well in my studies and then turned his attention to the next in line, leaving us free to check out the champagne bar. It was a brief encounter, but obviously one I will never forget. A lot is said about Prince Phillip, but on this occasion I found him to be jovial and,*

"Get him on a bad day and it's quite hard work. Get him on a good day, and you really don't want to be with anybody else"

Martin Palmer - theologian

despite all the regimented 'dos and don'ts' that go along with royal 'meet and greets'; he made me feel at ease. I will remember my short audience with him fondly.

Asked for her impressions of the Duke during a television documentary about him, actor Joanna Lumley described him as, "a bird of prey, a hawk or an eagle, there's something absolutely penetrating about the eyes, you feel like you're being scanned". She added: "You raise your game; you rather hope he'll like you."

"He always speaks his mind, sometimes not necessarily with a high degree of tact"

Countess Mountbatten - Cousin

Meanwhile broadcasting legend David Attenborough says: "He's formidable, he's daunting, partly because of his position, but also because he is a very considerable intellect. The first time I met him, it was absolutely clear that if you turned up and you hadn't mastered the papers, he would detect it very quickly and you would be in trouble."

As for theologian Martin Palmer, he admits that like most men, the Duke has his moments: "Get him on a bad day and it's quite hard work. Get him on a good day, and you really don't want to be with anybody else."

In the interview with Fiona Bruce to mark his 90th birthday, the Duke was as reluctant as he always has been to

trumpet his achievements. In answer to Ms Bruce's enquiry into why he thought he had been successful in his role he said, not without irritation, "I couldn't care less! Who cares what I think about it, I mean it's ridiculous."

Reluctance to talk about himself is, according to one of his sons, down to the Duke's modesty. "My father plain and simply is very modest about himself and doesn't believe in talking about himself," said Prince Edward, Earl of Wessex, in a television interview. "One of his best pieces of advice he gives to everybody is talk about everything else, don't talk about yourself - nobody's interested in you." And in the same vein, the Duke's cousin Lady Myra Butter says of him: "His motto is 'just get on with it'".

"He always speaks his mind, sometimes not necessarily with a high degree of tact," says his cousin Countess Mountbatten. "But on the other hand, I think that people have come to expect that of him, and they really rather enjoy it and they think, how nice to hear somebody actually say what they think."

But that's not to say that the Duke takes himself too seriously. Watching a gala performance of Sir Cameron Mackintosh's musical *Betty Blue Eyes* a few years ago in London's West End, he witnessed both himself and the Queen portrayed as part of the show. Played as comic turns, actor Dan Burton's first appearance on stage saw the Duke beaming, followed by gales of laughter as the young actor danced, in full naval uniform, as the young Prince Philip. Going backstage afterwards the Duke addressed Annalisa Rossi, the actress playing the Queen, saying: "You remind me of somebody…"

The Queen and Duke of Edinburgh at Trooping the Colour, June 2012.

Passions and pastimes

As for his passions, the Duke's boyhood love of sport continued into his adult life. Having ridden since childhood, he has always had a keen interest in horses and he took up polo while serving in Malta, playing regularly until the early 70s. He then began competing regularly in carriage-driving events. He has even represented Great Britain at several European and World Four-in-Hand Driving Championships.

President of the International Equestrian Federation from 1964 to 1986, he was involved in defining the rules and regulations for several equestrian sports. Under the Duke's auspices International Rules were created for Carriage Driving, Long Distance Riding and Vaulting, and Veterinary Committee and Veterinary Regulations were introduced.

Hosting the Royal Windsor Show in their back garden each year (since 1943, when it was created to raise money for the war effort) is a fixed point in the calendar for the Queen and the Duke. Although he stopped carriage driving himself when he was in his eighty-fifth year, it is still a sport that he enjoys watching. "If you've got a common interest no one cares a damn where you come from or who you are," said the Duke in response to a question from broadcaster Alan Titchmarsh about how sport brings people together.

In his younger days his love of the water saw him enjoying sailing and water-skiing. Having excelled at the sport at school, he also continued to play cricket.

The environment has also been a long-standing source of interest to Prince Philip. As well as using alternative energy sources for his official car, in the 1980s he used two electric Bedford vans to travel around London and has also used a Metrocab powered by LPG (liquid petroleum gas).

With a passion for conservation long before the rest of us had clocked the dangers of trashing vital habitats, the Duke, the first president of the World Wildlife Fund, was already taking a much longer view back in the 1950s. And in 2011 in a BBC interview he reiterated his concerns, saying: "If we've got this extraordinary diversity on this globe it seems awfully silly for us to destroy it. All these other creatures have an equal right to exist here, we have no prior rights to the Earth than anybody else and if they're here let's give them a chance to survive." He went on: "I think that there's a difference between being concerned for the conservation of nature and being a bunny hugger... people who simply love animals. People can't get their heads round the idea of a species surviving, you know, they're more concerned about how you treat a donkey in Sicily or something."

Art has also commanded the Duke's attention and interest. Having developed a genuine appreciation of fine art, the Duke is also a keen and talented artist in his own right. With a preference for painting in oils, his work includes a much celebrated candid portrait of the Queen having her breakfast in the dining room at Windsor Castle in the 1960s.

On the return trip from the Melbourne Olympics in 1956/57 the esteemed artist Edward Seago was personally invited by the Duke to accompany him aboard HMY *Britannia* for part of the trip, where the enthusiastic royal amateur no doubt benefited from Seago's talent and expertise.

Handy with a camera too, the Duke's

Portrait photo of Edward Seago (1910-1974)

personal photographs feature in his book *Birds from Britannia*. These shots were taken during the same trip with Seago, so the royal yacht must have been a hub of intensely creative activity on this particular voyage.

This splendid craft, alas decommissioned in 1997, was definitely one of the Duke's great passions – hardly surprising for a man who had so enjoyed his time in the Royal Navy.

In a commemorative book compiled to celebrate the forty-four years of HMY's life, the Duke wrote this as part of the book's foreword: 'Life has always been changing and things will not be the same now that *Britannia* is no longer in service.'

Launched by the Queen in April 1953, the idea was that *Britannia* would have a dual role. As well as enabling Her Majesty to have access to all the countries in the Commonwealth during peacetime, during wartime *Britannia* was to act as a hospital ship. Able to accommodate more than two hundred patients and some sixty staff, the

The bell on HMY Britannia

Royal Yacht Britannia The Royal Yacht Britannia was in Portsmouth for the 50th D-Day anniversary

iconic yacht – known only as Ship Number 691 until her name was made public – was kitted out with a dental surgery, operating theatre, X-ray department and a laboratory, with the Medical Director General of the Navy involved in the design right from the yacht's conception.

Although his interest wasn't in the vessel's medical aspect, Prince Philip was involved in the design and furnishing of *Britannia*. Asking endless questions, after the first set of designs for the interior of the royal apartments had been vetoed by the Queen on the grounds that they were too opulent and too expensive, the Duke brought in Sir Hugh Casson to take over. Continuing to have their say, the Queen and the Duke's personal tastes were very much in evidence in the end result.

But as well as fulfilling a practical role, *Britannia* also gave the Royal Family the one thing that was all too often in very short supply: privacy. Often used for royal holidays and honeymoons, life on board this beautiful craft surely offered a sense of freedom that must be hard to come by in day-to-day royal life.

Richard (Bill) Billinghurst was an electrical mechanic on the Royal Yacht *Britannia* from 1962 to 1969. Recalling both the Duke and *Britannia* fondly, freedom from the media spotlight is something that he touches on in this recollection:

He was a decent chap, the Duke of Edinburgh. He'd stop and talk to you and be friendly, but he was a naval officer as well as royalty so I didn't come into contact with him that often – we crew were quite separate from the royals. Mind you, Prince Philip was one for a laugh. We used to have a Crossing the Line ceremony whenever we crossed the Equator and once the Duke was on board when this happened. We all dressed up and he joined in by dressing up as one of The Beatles, with the wig and all. He could be very jovial. Although he would tear you off a strip if he caught you smoking – he hated smoking. The dining room on board Britannia *was always converted into a cinema when there was a new James Bond film out and the royal family used to enjoy watching these. Afterwards, we crew would get the chance to watch the films too.*

Prince Philip was usually on board with us for Cowes Week and every summer we would cruise around the Western Isles of Scotland. Britannia's *exact location on this trip was always a secret from the press so, if they wanted to, the royal family could take the Land Rover that we carried on board on to shore without anyone*

knowing where they might turn up. I think all the members of the Royal Family loved the privacy that being on board Britannia *gave them – they didn't have the press watching them all the time.*

Britannia *always sparkled. The brass portholes were always polished to a shine and the decks were scrubbed down every day. As crew, we had to wear white-soled gym shoes, which stopped the decks getting marked and kept the noise down for the royals.*

I know that Prince Philip had a lot to do with the design of the royal yacht and so I think he was especially happy on board."

Making no secret of his disagreeing with the decommissioning of *Britannia* ("she was as sound as a bell"), both the Duke and the Queen looked visibly stricken at the official decommissioning ceremony of their beloved home away from home.

Timed to coincide with his 90th birthday, *Prince Philip: Celebrating Ninety Years* was an exhibition held at the Windsor Castle Drawings Gallery.

Including early family photographs of him as a baby and toddler, loaned from the Duke's personal collection, as well as several photographs of him as a dashing young naval officer and snaps of the couple on their honeymoon in 1947, the exhibition also featured some of the Duke's own paintings, photographs and designs.

The Duke designed a stunning gold bracelet, given to the Queen on the occasion of their fifth wedding anniversary in 1952. It was decorated with the entwined letters E and P and featured an anchor, York roses and red, white and blue crosses. The exhibition also featured two sets of cufflinks designed by the Duke that were gifted to members of his staff who accompanied him on two royal tours.

Another exhibit was the work that brought his aptitude for design to public attention. Previously not at all widely known, it was the fire at Windsor Castle in 1992 that resulted in his talent being brought into the spotlight. The fire caused terrible damage – more than one hundred rooms were destroyed to the tune of £40 million, with the private chapel being one of the biggest casualties. Playing a leading role in the restoration project, the Duke designed a stained-glass window for the new chapel. Sketched on paper, the Duke's window is full of symbolism: a phoenix rising from the ashes to depict the restoration of Windsor Castle, St George slaying the dragon to represent the triumphing of good over evil and, perhaps even braver than St George, a fireman, complete with hose, tackling a blaze.

Science and technology is another area that has captured

Prince Philip's attention. Patron of the Industrial Society, now the Work Foundation, since 1952, in that time he has visited numerous laboratories, research stations and factories in order to see the real effects of scientific research for himself and to better understand industry. His patronages include several scientific-based organisations and he is a champion of engineering in education.

Home, as the saying goes, is where the heart is. For Prince Philip, home – or in his case homes – are another of his ongoing projects and his passions. After her accession to the throne, the Queen entrusted the overseeing of the running of Balmoral and Sandringham, private royal estates,

to the Duke. He is also Ranger of Windsor Great Park and played an active role in the team that undertook the monumental task of restoring the damaged parts of Windsor Castle after the dreadful fire of 1992.

Perhaps surprisingly, the Duke of Edinburgh is also said to be a keen reader of both poetry and spiritual books. T.S. Eliot, Shakespeare, Jung and the Bible are all to be found on his bookshelves, reflecting his interest in psychology, philosophy and religion.

Balmoral Castle

4 PATRONAGES & GOOD WORKS

Never could the Duke stand accused of being a slacker, but when it comes to patronages and good works, he is especially active. Patron of more than eight hundred organisations, some of these date back to shortly after his marriage.

One of his most long-standing associations was with the National Playing Fields Association (known as Fields in Trust since 2007) of which he was president. With a mission statement 'securing and improving outdoor space for sport and play for future generations', the Duke was an enthusiastic and hands-on supporter of the organisation. After sixty-four years dedication to the association, the Duke passed the presidency baton to the Duke of Cambridge, his grandson Prince William, in 2013. Set up in 1925 by King George V, this is one of the charitable organisations that has benefited from huge amounts of the Duke's energy and efforts. And despite ongoing pressure to get rid of playing fields, the number of fields protected by Fields in Trust protects more than 2,871 sites covering 28,865 acres. In a tribute to the Duke at the time of his passing the baton to his grandson Prince William, a spokesman said: "Without his help and contribution the organisation could not have achieved what it has done if, indeed, it would still have existed as an independent charity."

Other organisations in which the Duke has played a key role include the Federation of London Youth Clubs, The National Maritime Museum, The World Wildlife Fund, the

International Equestrian Federation, the Grand Order of Water Rats (an organisation of professional performers who raise money for charity), the Guinea Pig Club (the club for Second World War airmen who had plastic surgery after being badly burned) and the Hastings Winkle Club.

Another of his past patronages ties in with the Duke's affection for the sea. He has given two lengthy stints of service as President of the Royal Yachting Association; the first from 1956 to 1970, with the second lasting from 1975 to 1980.

But it is with the Duke of Edinburgh Award – of which more later – and the Prince Philip Designer's Prize, created in 1959 by the Duke as a response to post-war austerity, that he is perhaps most closely associated.

Starting life as the Duke of Edinburgh's Prize

THE DUKE OF EDINBURGH'S AWARD

A Duke of Edinburgh group on their expedition, 2008

for Elegant Design, the aim of the award was to acknowledge products that shone amid the practical and functional designs of the late 1950s. It seeks to celebrate elegant solutions to design problems. The Duke is a fan of problem-solving through design, as was shown during the television documentary about him in which he showed off his own design for a picnic trailer. Eminently practical, right down to the lack of 'rattle', he clearly has a keen interest in how things work. Genuinely curious when on visits to factories and production lines, he seizes the opportunity to ask questions about design and function in such an enthusiastic way that it seems unlikely that he is merely being polite.

He is Chairman of the judging panel himself, and winners of the Prince Philip Designer's Prize are selected based on the quality, originality and commercial success of their work, and the designer's overall contribution to the standing of design, and to design education.

The first winner was Charles Longman (the product was the brilliantly conceived Prestcold Packaway refrigerator, designed to be used in cramped kitchens). Since then the prize has recognised the very best products, graphics, buildings and engineering triumphs, showcasing designers' work and their contribution to innovation and excellence to modern life. James Dyson, Terence Conran and Kenneth Grange are all former winners of the Prize.

Commonwealth Study Conference

Another of the Duke's great achievements was the founding of the Commonwealth Study Conference. The first Commonwealth Study Conference was held in the UK in 1956 and was, according to the Duke, "an extraordinary experiment".

The conference is geared up to provide an opportunity for people from right across the Commonwealth, from all backgrounds, to come together and examine the relationship between industry and the community around it. The intent was not to reach any conclusions, but to challenge the participants' assumptions and prejudices; to present them with real situations and to see what the collective could learn from one another.

At the Duke's insistence, members had to be "people who appeared likely to be in the next generations of leaders, so that when the time came for them to take important decisions they would have the benefit of what they had discovered at the Study Conference to help them".

So useful was the inaugural conference that participants resolved to keep the conferences going, ensuring that future generations benefited from the same productive and insightful sharing of experience.

The Duke's brainchild has, since 1956, seen conferences

run at approximately six-year intervals. Hosted in Australia, Canada, India, Malaysia, New Zealand and the United Kingdom, the Commonwealth Study Conference was one of his most effective creations and an example of how resourceful and practical his mind is.

Now known as the Commonwealth Leadership Development Conferences and the Regional Dialogues, the Duke remains as the organisation's Patron. His daughter, Princess Anne, is now its President.

The Duke of Edinburgh Award

"One of the perpetual problems about human life is that young people of every generation have to discover for themselves what life is all about."

The Duke of Edinburgh

The triumvirate that formed the backbone of the Duke of Edinburgh Award comprised former headmaster of Gordonstoun and German educationalist Kurt Hahn, Lord Hunt, leader of the first successful ascent of Everest

expedition in 1953, and the Duke. Hahn was the driving force behind the scheme, determined to broaden out a badge that pupils at Gordonstoun strove to achieve. It's unlikely that he could have imagined back then that the scheme would become one of the world's most popular youth challenges.

The Award was initially set up in response to concerns about the development of boys in the wake of WW2. Leaving a gap between boys leaving school at 15 and entering National Service at 18, this three-year 'hole' left youngsters without guidance or support and it was felt that the Award could provide a focus and a valuable chance for character development. The Award comprised four sections: Rescue and Public Service Training, the Expedition, Pursuits and Projects, and Fitness.

Although only available to boys aged between 14 and 18 at the outset, such was the demand that a similar scheme for girls was rolled out in September 1958. In 1980 the upper age limit was extended to 24, and the four sections were revised to the current format: Service, Adventurous Journey, Skills and Physical Recreation.

The Award is also run in other countries across the

British Commonwealth under the title of the Duke of Edinburgh's Award International Association, with countries beyond the Commonwealth also adopting the Award. The guiding principles remain the same, wherever the Award is run. Focusing on personal development, not competition with others, the idea is that young people learn skills both practical and social.

Now operating in over 140 countries and territories, the Award is now also targeting those who have not previously had opportunities to develop themselves,

including young offenders, those with disabilities, street children and aboriginal communities. Typically modest about his significant involvement, His Royal Highness says he got involved simply because Hahn sent for him; he refuses to take any credit for it whatsoever. I don't run it - I've said it's all fairly second hand, the whole business. I mean, I eventually got landed with the responsibility or the credit for it. "I've got no reason to be proud of it. It's satisfying that we've set up a formula that works - that's it," he said in a television interview.

> ## "He is a genius with people, but with youngsters especially"
>
> *Kurt Hahn*

However, he admits that it took off in a way that pleased all concerned: "When the first trial of the Award was launched in 1956, no one had any idea quite what would happen. In the event it was an instant success, and the Award has been growing and expanding worldwide ever since." And of course, as he identifies himself, there are always new recruits coming through: "It's always relevant because there's always a new generation coming up for it".

What he doesn't mention is that he himself provides endless advice, support and encouragement to those who deliver the scheme.

Kurt Hahn once said of Prince Philip that he was 'a genius with people' but with youngsters especially. "He had the extraordinary ability to comprehend teenagers better than they did themselves," said Kurt.

Having achieved her Bronze, Silver and Gold doe medals in 1998, 2000 and 2001 respectively, Caroline Clarke is a big fan of the scheme.

The Duke of Edinburgh scheme teaches you many important life lessons. It really develops you as a person and brings out the best in people. Encouragement to always do more than you think you can and to see the good in others is invaluable. Developing skills and building new relationships with new people provides you with a great grounding as you go on in life. I particularly enjoyed the community aspect and for one of my awards I worked alongside the fire brigade and helped to create a radio advert to promote safety in the home.

It goes without saying that the outdoor expeditions teach you the most. Survival skills, endurance, trust, how to cope when faced with the unknown and most importantly a sense of humour! Walking in all sorts of weather conditions with your life on your back allows you to discover a side of yourself you never knew you had. It opens up doors for opportunities you may otherwise not have chance for. The sense of achievement is immense and I was lucky enough to have my Gold Award presented to me by the Duke of Edinburgh himself at St James's Palace. Such a warm character, he took time to speak to everyone in small groups and made each and every one of us feel proud. What more could you ask for?

I look at my Bronze, Silver and Gold medals and feel enriched by what I have achieved and the experiences I have encountered. Long may the scheme continue!

the Duke's advice to his own children was to get involved in schemes, charities or organisations only if they felt they had a genuine interest in the cause, or that they could bring something to it. This seems to be founded on his own experience and whatever criticism comes his way, on the issue of his dedication to the causes he supports, his commitment is unquestionable and the level of his involvement generally far more than merely a name on headed notepaper.

On reaching his 90th year Prince Philip said he was 'winding down' his involvement with some of the charities and organisations in which he was involved, but he remains

> "I reckon I've done my bit so I want to enjoy myself a bit now....It's better to get out before you reach the sell-by date."
> *Prince Philip*

Patron of the Duke of Edinburgh Award. "I reckon I've done my bit so I want to enjoy myself a bit now, with less responsibility, less frantic rushing about, less preparation, less trying to think of something to say. On top of that your memory's going, I can't remember names and things," he admitted in a televised interview. "It's better to get out before you reach the sell-by date."

With an estimated seven million young people in 132 countries having gained their Duke of Edinburgh Award it's fair to say that yes, sir, consider your 'bit' absolutely well and truly 'done'.

5 FRIENDS & FAMILY

"We live in what virtually amounts to a museum
– which does not happen to a lot of people."

the Duke of Edinburgh

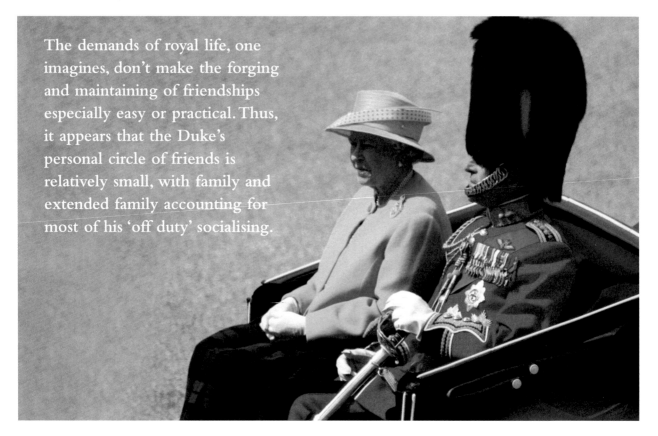

The demands of royal life, one imagines, don't make the forging and maintaining of friendships especially easy or practical. Thus, it appears that the Duke's personal circle of friends is relatively small, with family and extended family accounting for most of his 'off duty' socialising.

But over the years there have of course been those who have been close to the Duke. One man whom the Duke of Edinburgh had a long and close relationship with was Commander Michael Parker. Parker, who died in 2002, was the Duke's Private Secretary from 1948 to 1957, but the two men were, first and foremost, friends.

Both naval men, their first meeting was in 1942, when the Prince was just twenty-one years of age. Philip had just been appointed to the destroyer *Wallace* as a sub-lieutenant. With Parker holding the same position on board another ship in the fleet, *Lauderdale*, Parker and the Prince went into competition with one another, each trying to prove that their ship was better than the other's. It proved to be a bonding experience. Furthermore, Prince Philip found that as an Australian, Parker had a refreshing disregard for royal links. "I gave him deference when it was official, but if it was not official then 'relax' was the order of the day," Parker once said.

In 1947 the Prince told Parker that he was engaged to Princess Elizabeth. Parker was a guest at Prince Philip's stag night, which was held at the Dorchester Hotel in London. According to a well-documented story, after the press had

taken formal photographs of the groom-to-be and his guests, the 'stags' suggested that they should take pictures of the reporters. After this was done and the cameras had flashed, Mike Parker is said to have called out and, on cue, the camera bulbs were thrown, shattering against the wall. According to Mike Parker this was done in order to stop any snapper trying to take any more sneaky shots after the official photo call.

Shortly after the wedding, Prince Philip appointed Parker to the post of Equerry-in-Waiting to the Royal couple. A year later Parker was appointed to the newly-created post of the Duke of Edinburgh's Private Secretary.'

"He (the Duke) looked as if you'd dropped half the world on him"

Michael Parker's recollection of the Duke's reaction to the death of the Queen's father

King George VI is also reported to have liked the young Australian, so much so that he made it his business to help show the young courtier the royal ropes when it came to grasping the baffling ways of the court. He also took him

While the King may have helped him in matters of time-honoured tradition and royal custom, when it came to moving with the times Parker, like the Duke, was something of a moderniser. When the newlyweds moved into Buckingham Palace he set about having electric telephones installed and, in what must have been a joyous decision for those on royal pot wash duties, dishwashers were brought in.

During this time the Duke and Michael Parker continued to enjoy their friendship, occasionally winding up those who might not always have found their jokes so amusing. For instance, during an RAF manoeuvre over Buckingham Palace, they once telephoned the Air Ministry and played a recording of a Battle of Britain dogfight down the line, claiming that one of the pilots had gone bonkers and was attacking the Palace.

Parker and the Prince were also members of the Thursday Club, a luncheon club that met every Thursday in a private room at Wheeler's restaurant in Soho's Old Compton Street; members included actors David Niven and Peter Ustinov. Parker is reported to have said: "We enjoyed fun and going round with people who knew what

out shooting. And when the king died it was Parker who had to be the bearer of the bad news. On tour overseas with the royal couple, where they were staying at the Treetops Hotel in Kenya's Aberdare National Park, he broke the news to the Duke, who in turn had to tell his wife. "I never felt so sorry for anyone in all my life," Parker recalled, adding: "He (the Duke) looked as if you'd dropped half the world on him."

was going on." Finding it to be a highly effective way of keeping tabs on what was going on, Parker was quick to point out that while a good time was had by all, it was a generally well behaved gathering – "People got very merry, but never drunk".

It was Parker's divorce in 1958 that saw him forced to resign as the Duke's Private Secretary. This event generated many column inches and therefore reflected badly by association on the Royal Family. He left royal service to concentrate on a career in business.

But his friendship with the Duke never waned. Returning to his native Australia in the late 1960s, right up to the end of his life Parker kept in touch with Prince Philip. His letters began and concluded as they always had: 'Dear Philip… yours ever, Mike'.

Another close relationship, and one dating back to his boyhood, was with his uncle, Lord Mountbatten. Better known to the royal family as 'Uncle Dickie', Louis Francis Albert Victor Nicholas Mountbatten was born in Windsor on 25 June 1900. A German aristocrat and the Duke's mother's brother, Mountbatten will be forever remembered for being murdered by the IRA in August of 1979. Blowing

Earl Mountbatten of Burma in Naval Uniform

up a boat close to Mountbatten's holiday home in County Sligo, he was one of five victims killed in the horrific terrorist plot.

A respected British naval officer who was appointed the last Viceroy of British India and first Governor General of independent India, like Prince Philip, Mountbatten also attended the Royal Naval College at Dartmouth – indeed it was Mountbatten who persuaded his nephew to follow in the family tradition and join the Navy; Prince Philip's first choice had been the Air Force. Having seen action during WW1, in between the two wars Mountbatten continued his naval career, specialising in communications.

But to Prince Philip 'Uncle Dickie' became something of an unofficial guardian. Although Philip was originally closer to George, Mountbatten's older brother, when Georgie died Dickie took it upon himself to mentor the young Prince. According to Gyles Brandreth's book *Philip & Elizabeth*, Dickie, after a young Philip had stayed for a weekend, credits the Prince as being 'killingly funny', adding "I like him very much."

Continuing to be an influential figure throughout the Duke's life, Dickie also developed a very close relationship with the Duke's eldest son, Prince Charles. He was much loved by Charles, and was his confidant as well as his great uncle.

Mountbatten's funeral took place in Westminster Abbey and he was buried at Romsey Abbey, near Broadlands. At his great uncle's memorial service in December 1979, Prince Charles did not mince his words in making clear what he thought of those responsible for Mountbatten's murder, calling the type of man responsible 'the kind of subhuman extremist that blows people up when he feels like it'.

Head of the family: father

On November 14th 1948 broadcaster John Snagge was tasked with making an important late night announcement on the BBC: Princess Elizabeth 'was safely delivered of a prince'. Confirming that mother and baby were doing well and offering 'royal congratulations' on behalf of the listeners, Mr Snagge then no doubt pushed off to the nearest pub to wet the royal baby's head. Born at Buckingham Palace in the Belgian Suite, as were his brothers (Princess Anne was

born at Clarence House), labour had been long – thirty hours – and the Princess Elizabeth was understandably exhausted. So too was the Duke – he'd worked off his nervous energy by playing squash and swimming. As he was towelling himself dry after his dip, a footman arrived to tell him that he had just become a father. By the time his wife recovered from the anaesthetic that had been administered as pain relief, the Duke was at her side, brandishing celebratory champagne and flowers for the new mummy.

Philip was said to have read extensively to his children when they were small, including the poem *Hiawatha* – oh to have been a fly on the wall! When talking about her father in the ITV documentary *Prince Philip at 90,* Princess Anne recalled the Duke not only reading bedtime stories to her and her siblings when they were children, but also, with the Queen, playing chasing games. The Princess Royal also said that the Duke of Edinburgh and the Queen were happy to participate in games with their children in what the Princess described as a time when "families made their own play". According to the Princess, "They were both very quick."

The Princess Royal is widely regarded as the child most

like the Duke in terms of character and temperament, but his relationship with Prince Charles was less straightforward. "Charles is a romantic and I'm a pragmatist. That means we do see things differently," the Duke told royal biographer Gyles Brandreth during a conversation when the latter was researching his book on the Queen and the Duke's marriage.

But that is not to say that the Duke is insensitive – many recollections suggest absolutely otherwise – but one can see, perhaps, that the contrast between a sensitive son and a much more practical father could present difficulties in any family, never mind a royal family that has to live so much in the public eye. The Duke is not unkind, but he is not sentimental. In 1994, Charles revealed in his authorised biography (by Jonathan Dimbleby) that he felt 'emotionally estranged' from his parents. He added that he had longed for the level of affection that, he believed, they were 'unable or unwilling to offer'. His words caused his parents pain – and naturally they were not thrilled that he chose to make his criticisms of them publicly. But the Duke won't retaliate. Not publicly, at least, and he would only tell Brandreth that of their parenting skills, "we did our best."

Charles revealed in his authorised biography (by Jonathan Dimbleby) that he felt 'emotionally estranged' from his parents

Other memories of the Duke as a father from close friends recall him being hands on with go-karts, telling stories that he had dreamed up himself and jolly picnics, all with a distinct absence of tension and unhappiness.

But if things went wrong with the relationship between Charles and his parents it is perhaps the mix overall that is the biggest contributing factor. The different personality types of Charles and his father, the absence, on occasion, of the Duke who was part of a pairing which had a non-negotiable public duty to fulfil when Charles was small and the realisation early on that his sister, so much more like her father, clearly enjoyed a more relaxed relationship with the Duke than he did, must have been awkward for Philip and Elizabeth's firstborn.

Today, with both now considerably older, it seems that there is more warmth and understanding between them. At the Buckingham Palace concert to celebrate the Diamond Jubilee, from which the Duke was absent due to being admitted to hospital, Prince Charles urged the crowd to yell their good wishes loudly enough for his Pa to hear them a few miles down the road in his hospital bed.

But his parents are sometimes exasperated by Charles.

They are generally prudent when it comes to spending money (think of those Tupperware boxes keeping the royal cornflakes fresher for longer!), so Charles' tendency to extravagance is reputedly a bone of contention still.

It's fair to say that it probably hasn't been easy for the Queen, the Duke or their son. But like any parents they are nevertheless proud of their son's accomplishments. Although he never got to see active service, Prince Charles embraced military service and qualified as an RAF pilot, going on to embark upon a naval career. The Queen even singled him out and praised him publicly in a speech at Guildhall in

---

"Judging by some families, I think we are all on pretty good speaking terms after all this time"

Princess Royal

2002, during which she also paid tribute to her husband and all their children: 'the Duke of Edinburgh has made an invaluable contribution to my life over these past fifty years… 'We both of us have a special place in our hearts for our children. I want to express my admiration for the Prince

The Princess Royal

of Wales and for all he has achieved for this country'.

Unlike her brother, the Princess Royal won't say a word against her parents. Denying absolutely the assertion that the Queen and the Duke were unavailable, physically or emotionally, when she and her siblings were growing up, Anne is quoted as saying that the children were 'always encouraged to discuss problems, to talk them through'. And with the pragmatism of her father she is also on the record as saying: 'Judging by some families, I think we are all on pretty good speaking terms after all this time.'

As for his relationship with Prince Edward, Prince Philip seems also to find this easier. Although given his naval background one might imagine that he was less than chuffed when

HRH Prince Edward, the current Earl of Wessex

Edward bailed out of the Royal Marines (and Lord only knows what the Duke made of Edward's dalliance with theatrical types when he worked briefly for Lord Lloyd Webber's company The Really Useful Group!), his youngest son has, little by little, taken on a number of his father's responsibilities, most significantly that of helmsman for the Duke of Edinburgh Award. Edward, who will succeed his father as the new Duke of Edinburgh, is also the first of the Duke's children to pass on his name: Edward's eldest child, Louise, has the surname Mountbatten-Windsor.

the Duke of York, 2007

With his middle son, Andrew, Duke of York, the Duke of Edinburgh must have been, privately at least, proud to see him following in his footsteps and enrolling as a cadet at Dartmouth Royal Naval College. Andrew qualified as a helicopter pilot at just twenty-one, and his parents were immensely proud of his service to his Queen and country during the Falklands War. His subsequent ill-fated marriage to Sarah Ferguson, however, was not something that inspired the same pleasure.

And while Sophie Wessex, Edward's wife, may have proved herself to be a good wife, as a daughter-in-law she has been shockingly indiscreet and has no doubt given her royal in-laws good reason to grind their teeth – one can easily imagine the Duke's response to the bombshell that was Sophie's revelations to the *News of the World's* 'fake sheikh'.

Diana

Having been initially delighted when Prince Charles's engagement to Lady Diana Spencer was announced, when the marriage started to unravel the Queen and Prince Philip,

while they made no public comment, were reported to be both horrified and dismayed. Some years later it came to light that Prince Philip had done his best to help. As his son's marriage went into injury time, the Duke corresponded with his daughter-in-law, hoping to be of support and practical help. The tabloid press indicated that the Duke had written to Diana to tear her off a strip, and that he called her unkind names, including a harlot. This this was utter tosh. Gyles Brandreth reports that the Duke's letters to Diana were sympathetic, but direct, and always signed from

'Pa'. Likewise, royal biographer Hugo Vickers says: "I saw that correspondence between Prince Philip and the Princess of Wales and I hope one day that it will be published in full, because it was extremely moving and interesting on both sides and he made a very determined effort to find any way that he could to keep that marriage going. He shared with her quite a lot of his own experiences of what it was like for him marrying into the family and how that he too understood what she was going through."

The question of their son's second marriage to Camilla was another tricky one for the Duke and the Queen. Having established that the younger couple's relationship was initially adulterous, and with the scandal that was the 'Camillagate' sex tapes available to anyone who could face listening to them, time has, for the most part, healed the ire and sadness for all parties.

Grandfather

If celebrations for his 90th birthday are anything to go by then the Duke is a well-loved grandfather. As well as several formal 'dos' that marked the occasion, the final party was a merry and relaxed family meal that took place at a swanky Michelin-starred restaurant, the Waterside Inn in Bray.

Organised by his grandchildren – who also picked up the tab – the meal was attended by Prince William and the Duchess of Cambridge, Princesses Beatrice and Eugenie, Zara Phillips and her brother Peter and his wife Autumn. Only Prince Harry, who had a prior engagement, was absent.

But possibly, like many, the Duke has had the rehearsal of parenthood in which to learn from his mistakes, making

being a grandparent an easier role for him. Or perhaps it is the advantage of being 'one place removed' that many grandparents find enables them to have a close and more open relationship with their younger generation? Either way, nobody will forget the deeply touching support he gave to William and Harry at their mother's funeral. Prince Charles, Diana's ex-husband, and her brother, Charles Spencer, were expected to walk behind the gun carriage carrying Diana's coffin to Westminster Abbey. The young Princes Harry and William were far from sure that they wanted to walk behind the coffin, especially William. Royal

biographer Hugo Vickers revealed in a television documentary about the Duke that Prince Philip advised William thus: "I think when you are older you might very much regret not walking behind your mother's coffin." And although he had not initially planned to do so, he added: "If I walk, will you walk with me?"

Of course one can only guess, but it seems likely that having the support of their grandfather on this most difficult of occasions must have been of real comfort to the young boys.

It seems that earlier that same week the Duke, incandescent with rage, had directed his anger at Labour spin doctors who were trying to dictate the arrangements for the funeral, including what they thought William and Harry should do. Describing events leading up to the funeral in his memoirs, Sky News Political Editor Adam Boulton recalls: 'Blair had been helpful reading the public mood when Diana had died, but he was also presumptuous.' Going on to tell how spin doctors visited Buckingham Palace and tried to organise what roles Harry and William should take in the funeral, the Duke, who was listening via speakerphone from Balmoral, lost his royal cool and yelled: 'F★★★ off! We are talking about two boys who have lost their mother.'

Parent or grandparent, rumour has it that the Duke is a bit of a natural with little ones. There are several accounts that describe him as being good with children and babies – even Cherie Blair, the wife of the former Prime Minister, credits the Duke with being brilliant with little ones. Evidently when the Blairs went to stay at Balmoral, with their youngest child, Leo, who was two at the time, the young man amused the Duke hugely by singing the entire first verse of the National Anthem. Not to be outdone, Philip promptly sang the second verse. And according to Countess Mountbatten, Prince Philip has always enjoyed the company of children and they have always been taken with him. Now, with great-grandchildren coming along, one suspects that chasing games might be a tad slower than they were when the Duke's own children were little.

6 RIGHT ROYAL RANDOMS:

the Duke by facts and stats

The Duke of Edinburgh's birthplace was his parents' house Mon Repos on the island of Corfu. The house had been the country residence of the British High Commissioner for the Ionian Islands.

The Duke has outlived all of his four older sisters. Tragedy struck Cecilie; in 1937 she and her husband and two sons were killed in an air crash. Theodora died in 1969, followed by Margarita in 1981. Sophie lived longest of the four princesses, passing away in 2001.

Since 1952, the Duke has made more than 600 solo visits to 143 countries.

In addition to many foreign decorations, he has received honorary degrees from a number of universities. A former Chancellor of the Universities of Cambridge, Edinburgh, Wales and Salford, he is also a Life Governor of King's College at the University of London. When he was invited to become Chancellor of the University of Wales in 1948, one of his first acts was to present the Queen, then Princess Elizabeth, with an honorary degree. This entailed him having to recite in Welsh.

Prince Philip was the first member of the Royal Family to be interviewed on television. The interview took place in May 1961 and *Question Time's* Richard Dimbleby was asking the questions.

With no constitutional role other than as a Privy Counsellor, Prince Philip does not read state papers or other official documents which the Queen receives from her governments. He doesn't get invited to join the Queen when she has an audience with her ministers either.

Until 2011, when last recorded, Prince Philip carried out an average of more than 350 engagements each year.

The Duke's grandmother and mother were born in the same room in Windsor Castle. The Duke was once taken by his grandmother to have afternoon tea with her aunt Beatrice, Queen Victoria's youngest daughter.

While at Dartmouth Naval College, as well as the King's Dirk for being the as best all-round cadet of his term, the Duke was also a recipient of the Eardley-Howard-Crockett Prize for the Best Cadet. This prize came in the form of a £2 book token.

When planning their wedding, the Queen and Prince Philip had to wait to get hitched until after the Royal Tour of South Africa, in which the bride-to-be was involved.

The first Duke of Edinburgh, Prince Philip's great-great uncle, Prince Alfred, also had a successful naval career. He retired as Admiral of the Fleet in 1893.

The Duke learned to fly with the RAF and gained his RAF Wings in 1953. He gained his helicopter wings with the Royal Navy in 1956, and his Private Pilot's Licence in 1959. He was Grand Master of the Guild of Air Pilots and Air Navigators from 1952 until 2002.

By the time he gave up flying in 1997 the Duke had notched up 5,986 hours as a pilot in 59 types of aircraft in 44 years.

From 1952-1999 the Duke was President of the Royal Mint Advisory Committee for the Design of Coins, Seals and Medals.

The Duke is Patron of the Friends of the Royal Academy of Arts.

When the Duke retired from polo in 1971 he did so with a handicap of 5. He played a key part in setting up the Household Brigade (now Guards) Polo Club on Smith's Lawn in Windsor Great Park. The Duke also set up the Windsor Park Equestrian Club, also on Smith's Lawn.

When the Duke took up competition carriage driving he borrowed a team of four carriage horses from the Royal Mews. A member of the British team, he attended several World and European Championships and won one World Team gold, three World Team bronze medals and one European Team bronze.

The Duke was President of the Football Association from 1955 to 1958.

While many books have been written about him, Prince Philip has written several himself. The subjects span carriage driving, the environmental revolution, dressage and wildlife.

Returning from the Olympic Games in Melbourne in 1956 the Duke sailed across the South Pacific in *Britannia*, the Royal Yacht, stopping off at several points along the way, before meeting the Queen for a state visit to Portugal.

Having a particular interest in the conservation of nature and the natural environment, in 1960 the Duke, together with Lord Buxton, initiated the first of three 'Countryside in 1970' conferences.

During his involvement with the National Maritime Museum, Prince Philip, in collaboration with the Museum's Director, Frank Carr, formed the Cutty Sark Trust in a bid to save the famous tea clipper from the breakers' yard. The Trust raised the money to purchase the ship, build a dry dock at Greenwich and restore her.

The Duke and Frank Carr also established the Maritime Trust, in order to save and preserve historic ships. The Trust has been responsible for saving several significant ships, including Brunel's SS *Great Britain*, HMS *Warrior* and Henry VIII's *Mary Rose*.

When fire caused severe damage to part of Windsor Castle, the Duke was in Buenos Aires chairing the World Wildlife Fund Annual Conference. As the House of Commons declined to vote any funds for the restoration of the Castle, the Royal Household, under the direction of the then

Keeper of the Privy Purse, Sir Michael Peat, agreed to raise the money needed for repair and restoration. Opening Buckingham Palace to the public and charging an admission fee was of significant help in funding the repair work.

The Duke has many military associations. In 1953, he was appointed Captain General of the Royal Marines. He was appointed Colonel-in-Chief of the Queen's Own Cameron Highlanders, the 8th King's Royal Irish Hussars and the Wiltshire Regiment in 1952. The Wiltshire Regiment was amalgamated with the Royal Berkshire Regiment to form the Duke of Edinburgh's Royal Regiment. Subsequent amalgamations have turned these regiments into the 4th Battalion of the Regiment of Scotland, the Highlanders; the Queen's Royal Hussars; and the 1st Battalion, the Rifles. He is also Colonel-in-Chief of the Royal Electrical and Mechanical Engineers, and of the Intelligence Corps. He is Colonel-in-Chief of the Royal Canadian Regiment and of the Australian Electrical and Mechanical Engineers. He is also Honorary Colonel of the Trinidad and Tobago Regiment.

The Duke was appointed Colonel of the Welsh Guards in 1953. He handed them over to his son, the Prince of Wales, in 1975. He was then appointed Colonel of the Grenadier Guards, the senior regiment of the Foot Guards.

The Duke is an Honorary Fellow of the Royal College of Surgeons of England, and of Edinburgh. He is Patron of the London School of Hygiene and Tropical Medicine.

When Kurt Hahn, his Gordonstoun headmaster and the school's founder died in 1974, Prince Philip read the story of the Good Samaritan in the lesson at his memorial service. The Duke also has a collection of original political and royal cartoons. This follows in the footsteps of Kings George III and George IV, whose collections are now held by the Library of Congress.

Buckingham Palace narrowly missed severe bomb damage during the Second World War. The only significant damage was to the Private Chapel.

In 2010 a former spy claimed that the IRA once tried to assassinate Prince Philip. Australian journalist and former spy Warner Russell told of how two bombs were planted in Sydney in 1973, with the target being the Duke of Edinburgh's cortège. Both devices were found, one in a bin and the other in a locker at Central Station, just moments before the Duke was scheduled to pass that way, prompting an immediate security operation. The Duke, fifty-one at the time, was visiting the country to officiate at the opening of an RAF memorial in Canberra. Russell, who at the time was working for a newspaper, says that he took a telephone call the day before, warning of the attack. Passing on details of the threat to someone he knew in Intelligence, Russell also claims that the Australian government prevented the details leaking out to the media in order to keep the plot from members of the public. However, a brief story later appeared in the *New York Times* detailing the discovery of the bombs.

As he has so often been called upon to make speeches, the Duke's collected speeches cover over a yard of shelf space. It is thought he has made more than 5,000 speeches in his public life to date.

He has been the recipient of many gifts over the years. The more unusual include a pair of live pigmy hippopotami from President Tubam of Liberia and a giant porcelain grasshopper wine-cooler from President Pompidou of France.

The bracelet that Prince Philip presented to the Queen as a wedding present was his own design.

A salute of 41 guns is fired on the Duke's birthday by the King's Troop Royal Artillery in Hyde Park, and the Union flag is flown from government buildings on that day.

The Duke's Standard consists of four quarters: the three lions and hearts from the Danish Royal coat of arms; the white cross on a blue background from the Greek national flag; the black and white stripes from the Battenberg coat of arms; and Edinburgh Castle from the City of Edinburgh's coat of arms. He chose Edinburgh Castle surmounted by a Ducal Coronet and surrounded by the Garter as his 'Badge', and green as his 'livery' colour.

All the Duke's cars have been painted 'Edinburgh Green'. When occasion demands it, the Duke wears the kilt. In uniform it is the relevant regimental tartan. For 'plain clothes' he opts for either the Balmoral or the Royal Stewart tartan.

The Duke is a spiritual man. A committed Christian, as President of the WWF, and in conjunction with Martin Palmer, in 1986, he organised a meeting between leaders of the major faiths during WWF's 25th anniversary conference in Assisi.

The Duke has turned his hand to garden design. He redesigned the layout of the gardens on the East Terrace of Windsor and designed the fountain. He also created the private garden under the south wall of the Castle. He has, over time, redesigned the gardens at Balmoral, which has included the creation of a water garden. Using a bulldozer for the job, he dug out the plot himself.

The Duke was closely involved with every aspect of the design of the Royal Yacht *Britannia*.

As an ex-serviceman of the Second World War, the Duke has a keen interest in his fellow ex-servicemen. He took over as Grand President of the Royal Commonwealth Ex-Services League from his uncle Earl Mountbatten of Burma in 1974.

The Silver Wink Trophy is one of many cups, medals and prizes, associated with the Duke. Dating back to 1958 when some students at Cambridge challenged the Duke to a tiddlywinks match, the Duke nominated the comedy team the Goons as his Champions. The Duke designed and had made a special Silver Wink trophy which is presented annually to the winning team of the inter-University Tiddlywinks Championship.

The Duke was the first member of the Royal Family ever to fly out of Buckingham Palace Garden in a helicopter.

In 1959 the Duke flew to Ghana via Palma in a de Havilland Heron. En route, he spent the night in El Golea in the middle of the Sahara.

The Duke has eight grandchildren. They are: Peter Phillips, Zara Phillips, Prince William, Prince Harry, Princess Beatrice, Princess Eugenie, Lady Louise Windsor and James, Lord Severn. Peter and Autumn Phillips gave him his first great-grandchild, Savannah, in 2010. Prince William and the Duchess of Cambridge presented him with his second great-grandchild, Prince George, in 2013. His third, born to Zara Phillips and her husband Mike Tindall, was a baby girl, Mia, born in 2014.

The Duke is the oldest living great-great-grandchild of Queen Victoria.

The Duke had an early version of a mobile telephone, made by Pye Telecommunications of Cambridge. This was fitted to his car in 1953.

Having previously owned an Apricot computer in the early 1980s, the Duke now uses a laptop.

The Duke was Chairman of the Westminster Abbey Trust, which raised the money for and supervised the restoration of the fabric of the Abbey between 1973 and 1997. When the Abbey determined to fill empty recesses above the Great West Door with figures of modern saints, the Grand Duchess Elizabeth of Russia, one of the Duke's great aunts, was one of those selected.

The Duke played a part in creating the Windsor Farm Shop. Opened in 2001, it sells a range of produce including meat, eggs, fruit and vegetables, all harvested from the Sandringham Estate.

In 2009, the Duke became the longest-serving consort in British history when he outlived Queen Charlotte, the wife of King George III.

On a visit with the Queen to Lloyds of London in 2014, the Duke jokingly enquired whether the Royal Collection was insured for damage caused by mice. Keen to ensure that financial cover for all the priceless royal treasures was sufficient, whether it was a palace puss not pulling his or her weight in mouse disposal that prompted the Duke's question is not known. However, having been collected by sovereigns over many years, and including works of art by the likes of Vermeer and Rembrandt, as well as contemporary artists such as Tracey Emin and Lucian Freud, the royal collection is likely to need a pretty comprehensive policy.

Dining with the Duke

Due to rationing, the wedding cake baked to celebrate the Queen and Prince Philip's marriage was made using ingredients that were offered as a wedding present by the Australian Girl Guides. The royal bakers of the cake were McVitie & Price.

Gaelic steaks, the recipe for which includes a smear of Marmite, are said to be one of the Duke's favourite dishes.

A big fan of barbecued food, the Duke of Edinburgh was once filmed (for the 1969 documentary The Royal Family) grilling steaks at Balmoral on a griddle he had designed himself. When game is shot at Balmoral the Duke would ask chefs to marinate the finer cuts so that he could barbecue them the same evening. Joints that weren't deemed top-notch would be used for stewing and served at the next shooting lunch. Other less impressive cuts would be sent to the village butcher to be made into sausages.

At one time, if Prince Philip had an opinion on a particular wine served at he would write his verdict on the bottle label.

Hale and hearty

Having enjoyed rude health for most of his life, it is only really in recent years that Prince Philip has been troubled by illness. Just shy of his ninety-second birthday, in 2013 he was admitted to a London Clinic for what was described as an exploratory operation on his abdomen. Typically, the Duke didn't let his impending hospitalisation interfere with the usual business of royal life any more than strictly necessary. He was admitted directly after a Buckingham Palace garden party, at which guests claim that he gave no indication of being poorly, and discharged eleven days later. After a short period of convalescence he undertook his first public engagement on 12 August. Announcing that it was "a great pleasure to be back in circulation again", the Duke was reported to be cheerful and in good spirits as he handed out medals at The Royal Society of Edinburgh.

In 2012 the Duke was also under the doctor, having been taken to hospital after the recurrence of a bladder infection, which had previously seen him missing out on some of the Queen's Diamond Jubilee celebrations and being treated at London's King Edward Vll hospital. Having stood with the Queen on the royal barge for almost two hours, in typically British drizzle, as a flotilla of boats sailed down the Thames to Tower Bridge, by the time the big Diamond Jubilee concert took place, featuring some of the music industry's most famous names, the Duke was tucked up in a hospital bed. It's probably safe to say that if he had to miss any element of the celebrations, a (mostly) pop concert would have been his choice!

The Duke had a minor operation in 2010 in relation to carpal tunnel syndrome, a relatively common condition that causes pain and numbness. In December 2011 doctors performed what was referred to by a Buckingham Palace spokesman as a 'minimally invasive procedure of coronary stenting' (this would be to improve arterial blood flow). He was admitted as a day patient and was soon back in harness, having missed an evening dinner engagement and a royal visit to Crewe.

We'll meet again...

In November 2013 the Duke was reunited with an airman he had help to rescue in the Pacific. Visiting the Royal British Legion's Field of Remembrance at Westminster Abbey accompanied by grandson Prince Harry, he was reintroduced to former Petty Officer Norman Richardson, who in 1945 was scooped up by the Duke's ship HMS *Whelp* after he was shot down by a Japanese Zero fighter. Evidently the Duke lent Mr Richardson a set of his clothes after his rescue. Now in his 90s like the Duke, Mr Richardson was one of several veterans that the Duke spoke to at the site, where 100,000 crosses are planted by families of the fallen. Delighted to meet the Duke again, Mr Richardson said: "We had a joke about Prince Philip giving me a set of his clothes when I was picked up off the coast of Sumatra. The Duke still remembers it, and I told him they weren't really his clothes, they were the property of the purser's store."

The decorated Duke

Seen festooned with medals in November 2013 at the opening of the new headquarters of the SSAF (formerly known as the Soldiers, Sailors, and Airmen Families Association), it was a reminder that the Duke of Edinburgh has been well decorated over the years.

Sporting seventeen medals and decorations on this occasion, the Duke of Edinburgh had donned the impressive array of military awards as he accompanied the Queen to open charity's new base at Queen Elizabeth House in central London in accordance with the charity's request that all guests wear medals.

Including the Greek War Cross of Honour, awarded for his bravery in the Battle of Cape Matapan against the Italian Navy in 1941, the Duke's medals include:

Queen's Service Order, New Zealand - Awarded by the Government of New Zealand for service to the country, the medal is shaped like a flower.

1939-1945 Star - A campaign medal of the British Commonwealth awarded for service during the Second World War.

Atlantic Star - Awarded in 1945 for his service in the Atlantic during the Second World War.

Africa Star - Awarded in 1945 for service in Africa during the Second World War.

Burma Star - Awarded for service in the Burma Campaign in the Second World War.

Italy Star - Awarded for service in Italy and surrounding areas in the Second World War.

War Medal 1939-1945, with Mention in Dispatches - Awarded to those who served in the Armed Forces or Merchant Navy for at least 28 days between1939-45. An oak leaf featured on the ribbon denotes the Mention in Dispatches.

King George VI Coronation Medal, 1937 - these medals were created to commemorate the coronation of King George VI and Queen Elizabeth.

Queen Elizabeth II Coronation Medal, 1953 - A commemorative medal made to celebrate the coronation of Queen Elizabeth II.

Queen Elizabeth II Silver Jubilee Medal, 1977 - A commemorative medal created in 1977 to mark the Queen's Silver Jubilee.

Queen Elizabeth II Golden Jubilee Medal, 2002 - A commemorative medal created in 2002 to mark the 50th anniversary of the Queen's accession to the throne.

Queen Elizabeth II Diamond Jubilee Medal, 2012 - A commemorative medal created last year to mark the 60th anniversary of the Queen's accession to the throne.

Canadian Forces Decoration - An honorary award presented to the Duke in April 2013.

New Zealand Commemoration Medal, 1990 - Awarded only during 1990 to some 3,000 people in recognition of contributions made to New Zealand life.

Malta George Cross 50th Anniversary Medal, 1992 - A commemorative medal awarded by, or in the name of, the President of Malta.

Greek War Cross, 1950 - Awarded for heroism in wartime to both Greeks and foreign allies. The Duke earned this medal for his bravery in fighting the Italians when they invaded Greece in 1941.

Croix de Guerre (France) with Palm, 1948 - A French military decoration to honour people who fought with the Allies against Axis nations in the Second World War.

In 2014 the 92-year-old Duke of Edinburgh was voted on to *GQ's* list of best-dressed men of the year. Taking 26th place, the Duke found himself in the sartorial company of singers, actors, newsreaders, footballers and models. A

spokesperson for the magazine said that Philip "deserves yet another medal - for his services to classic British tailoring".

Putting one's foot in it

"You have mosquitos. I have the Press."

The Duke of Edinburgh (To the matron of a hospital in the Caribbean)

As far as the press goes it is clear that the Duke feels that he is often misrepresented. But he was the one to recognise that the Royal Family had to let the press in, at least a little way, if the monarchy were to survive. The first member of the family to appear on television, in 1969 he also agreed to a film that depicted his family 'at home'.

But undoubtedly, even though he is always at pains to ensure that photographers get the all the pictures they need at official line-ups, he knows that there will always be a thirst for something more than is offered: the recording of a quote that was part of a private conversation, an unscheduled picture or, more worryingly recently, the possibility that private telephone calls are being overheard by hackers who just happen to be hacks.

Resigned rather than bitter, the Duke said during a television interview in 2011 that "media is a professional intruder. You can't complain." Which, given the often untrue and unkind treatment he and his family have been on the receiving end of, is pretty big of him. And in an interview with *The Independent* in 1992 he said: "I don't hate the press; I find a lot of it is very unpalatable. But if that's the way they want to behave, well..."

As for many of his so called 'gaffes', it is important to remember that many of these have been taken out of context and in some cases have been completely untrue. Again, the Duke seldom reacts publicly. And the truth of the matter is that the intent behind his sometimes misplaced or mistimed comments is nothing but good. Certainly his humour might sometimes be inappropriate, but this is more likely to be a generational ignorance rather than based on any desire to be offensive.

It is said that when faced with a roomful of people, or a line up, that he endeavours to make at least one person laugh. As the star of the show the Queen doesn't have to make people laugh or say more than a few pleasant words to the people she meets in her line of duty – that she is there is enough. The Duke, meanwhile, perpetually tasked to walk two paces behind her, or even when he's appearing in his own right, is expected to perform. Therefore he's always having to scratch about for something to say that will convey that he is genuinely interested. This gives scope for getting it wrong sometimes. And when a big chunk of your job is shaking endless hands and making endless speeches, that scope is even greater. If you expect a seal to perform day in and day out, don't be surprised if he sometimes drops the ball. Or in the Duke's case, a clanger. Naturally the press greet any faux pas with the same degree of enthusiasm that the corgis might greet the leftovers of a state banquet.

But wouldn't we rather have a senior member of royalty who was warm, funny and, most importantly of all, human? If he didn't occasionally put his foot in it, the Duke wouldn't be nearly so real or so easy to relate to. Likely to call a spade a bloody shovel, yes - he is blunt. But from all that has been written about him over the years it is clear that he is not a deliberately unkind man. The following 'gaffes' are therefore those that have previously been reported in the national press. Their accuracy cannot be guaranteed, but if they were accurate, you can be sure they were not intended to cause offence.

Poking fun at himself when addressing the General Dental Council in 1960:

"Dontopedalogy is the science of opening your mouth and putting your foot in it, a science which I have practised for a good many years."

On the rate of British tax in 1963:

"All money nowadays seems to be produced with a natural homing instinct for the Treasury."

Incurring the wrath of British women everywhere in 1966:

"British women can't cook".

What the Duke said to Tom Jones after the latter's
Royal Variety Performance of 1969:

"What do you gargle with, pebbles?" (Later adding: *"It is very
difficult at all to see how it is possible to become immensely
valuable by singing what I think are the most hideous songs."*)

On the Royal Family's finances in 1969:

*"We go into the red next year. I shall probably have to
give up polo."*

During the recession in 1981:

*"Everybody was saying we must have more leisure. Now they
are complaining they are unemployed."*

Ill-timed for sure, talking to survivors
of the Lockerbie bombing:

*"People usually say that after a fire it is water damage that is the
worst. We are still drying out Windsor Castle."*

On viewing the plans for the Duke and then
Duchess of York's house at Sunninghill Park
(one doesn't like to ask how he might know...):

"It looks like a tart's bedroom."

Stereotyping or teasing? In Oban, Scotland in 1995
he asked a Scottish driving instructor:

*"How do you keep the natives off the booze long
enough to pass the test?"*

Following the Dunblane massacre in 1996, the Duke had his own views on the call to ban firearms:

"If a cricketer, for instance, suddenly decided to go into a school and batter a lot of people to death with a cricket bat, which he could do very easily, I mean, are you going to ban cricket bats?"

Undeniably irascible, frustrated by an aged car park attendant who failed to recognise him at Cambridge University in 1997:

"You bloody silly fool!"

Managing to insult both chorus girls and our friends from across the pond in the same breath in 2000 (but one suspects with his tongue firmly in his cheek):

"People think there's a rigid class system here, but dukes have been known to marry chorus girls. Some have even married Americans."

Setting a group of female Labour MPs chuntering at a drinks party at Buckingham Palace in 2000 and clearly with mischief in mind:

"Ah, so this is the feminist corner then."

Putting Elton John in his place in 2001:

"Oh it's you that owns that ghastly car is it? We often see it when driving to Windsor Castle."

Doing an unintentional impression of Basil Fawlty in 2002 while touring a factory near Edinburgh and in reference to a fuse box that he thought so crude that it:

"looked as though it had been put in by an Indian".

Almost stand-up material, in 2002, the Duke is reported as saying to a wheelchair-bound lady with a guide dog:

"Do you know they have eating dogs for the anorexic now?"

A tad swanky on a visit to the Aircraft Research Association in 2002:

"If you travel as much as we do, you appreciate the improvements in aircraft design of less noise and more comfort, provided you don't travel in something called economy class, which sounds ghastly."

Meanwhile, back at the Royal Variety Show in 2009 the Duke is ever politically correct when greeting the black dance troupe Diversity:

"Are you all one family?"

A hairy moment with a young fashion designer at Buckingham Palace in 2009:

"You didn't design your beard too well, did you? You really must try better with your beard."

Saucy in 2010 when, on asking a female Sea Cadet what she did for a living, and being told that she worked in a nightclub as a barmaid, the Duke asked her if it was a strip club. Registering her surprise, he dismissed the suggestion, saying that it was:

"probably too cold for that anyway".

On being told by a girl at a prize-giving ceremony for the Duke of Edinburgh Awards in 2010 that she'd been to Romania to help in an orphanage:

"Oh yes, there's a lot of orphanages in Romania - they must breed them".

On approaching his 90th birthday in 2011:
"Bits are beginning to drop off".

To the managing director of a wind farm company
on the subject of wind turbines in 2011:
"absolutely useless" and "an absolute disgrace".

Meeting a disabled man in 2012:
*"How many people have you knocked over this morning
on that thing?"*

Playing down his day job when being
interviewed by Jeremy Paxman:
"Any bloody fool can lay a wreath at the thingamy."

Discussing the tartan designed for the Papal visit with
then-Scottish Tory leader Annabel Goldie in 2013:
"That's a nice tie… do you have any knickers in that material?"

On the youth of today at the 50th anniversary of the
Duke of Edinburgh Awards scheme:
*"Young people are the same as they always were. They are just
as ignorant."*

On viewing an exhibition of primitive
Ethiopian art in 1965:
*"It looks like the kind of thing my daughter would bring back
from her school art lessons."*

In response to being asked if he would like to visit the Soviet Union in 1967:
"I would like to go to Russia very much, although the bastards murdered half my family."

On a 1976 tour of Canada:
"We don't come here for our health. We can think of other ways of enjoying ourselves."

When accepting a figurine from a woman during a visit to Kenya in 1984:
"You are a woman, aren't you?"

Advice to a British student in China in 1986:
"If you stay here much longer, you will go home with slitty eyes."

Observing in 1986 at a World Wildlife Fund meeting:
"If it has got four legs and it is not a chair, if it has got two wings and flies but is not an aeroplane and if it swims and it is not a submarine, the Cantonese will eat it."

Charming the pants of a BBC journalist at a banquet at the Elysée Palace after she asked Queen Elizabeth if she was enjoying her stay in Paris in 2006:
"Damn fool question!"

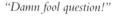

The Chinese tourist board is surely glad that Trip Advisor didn't exist back in 1986. Airing his views on Beijing, during a tour of China, the Duke was succinct and to the point:
"Ghastly."

Insults aren't just reserved for humans. On a visit to Australia in 1992 the Duke refused to stroke a koala bear:

"Oh no, I might catch some ghastly disease."

Making friends with a British tourist in Hungary in 1993:

"You can't have been here that long — you haven't got a pot belly."

Endearing himself to the natives by addressing an islander in the Cayman Islands in 1994:

"Aren't most of you descended from pirates?"

Advising a Caribbean rabbit breeder in Anguilla on the best way to promote pregnancy for bunnies in 1994:

"Don't feed your rabbits pawpaw fruit — it acts as a contraceptive. Then again, it might not work on rabbits."

Straight to the point in 1988 when meeting a British student who had been trekking in Papua New Guinea:

"You managed not to get eaten then?"

Stunning guests at the opening reception of a new £18million British Embassy in Berlin in 2000:

"It's a vast waste of space."

Down with kids: indicating to a 14-year-old in a Bangladeshi youth club in 2002:

"So who's on drugs here?... HE looks as if he's on drugs."

Clearly preferring grain to grape, when offered fine Italian wines by Giuliano Amato, the former Prime Minister, at a dinner in Rome in 2000:

"Get me a beer. I don't care what kind it is, just get me a beer!"

Visiting Australian Aborigines during a visit to Australia with the Queen in 2002:

"Do you still throw spears at each other?"

When shown the piezometer water gauge demonstrated by an Australian farmer in 2000 the Duke mischievously rechristens it:

"A pissometer?"

Chatting with President Barack Obama and in response to the President's comment that he had met with the leaders of the UK, China and Russia:

"Can you tell the difference between them?"

Commenting on the President of Nigeria's traditional robes:

"You look like you're ready for bed!"

And finally…

In February 2014 the Duke of Edinburgh made the headlines – this time through no fault of his own. While he was visiting the 1st Battalion Grenadier Guards at Aldershot, a football match between soldiers was taking place. One player complained bitterly after he was substituted in a game between corporals and guardsmen. Gasping with pain and doubled up with exhaustion on the touchline, the soldier was seemingly oblivious to the fact that the Duke was standing just a few feet away and proceeded to curse his way through a colourful range of swear words.

Asking if he was all right, the Duke got a swift response. "No, I'm f★★★★★," answered the soldier, who, still doubled over, was unaware of who was speaking to him.

As a naval man it is fair to assume that Prince Philip is unlikely to have been shocked by the language – indeed press reports suggest that he laughed! The injured player then raised his head and realised that it was in fact the Duke at whom he had just sworn. Evidently he shuffled off as fast as his exhausted legs could carry him.

Moderniser, grafter, character, devoted husband and loyal subject, the Duke has made an exceptionally difficult job look deceptively easy. He may have made mistakes along the way, but as he said to television presenter Alan Titchmarsh during an interview pegged to his 90th birthday celebrations: "I'd rather not have made the mistakes that I did make – but I'm not going to tell you what they are!"

Never showing off about what he does, or complaining about the workload that his role entails, he has, in his own words, 'just got on with it'. Long may he continue to do so.

Useful links

The Duke of Edinburgh Award - www.dofe.org

The Commonwealth Study Conferences - www.csc-alumni.org

The official website of the British Monarchy - www.royal.gov.uk

Fields in Trust (formerly The National Playing Fields Association) - www.fieldsintrust.org

Visit Britannia - www.royalyachtbritannia.co.uk

ND - #0038 - 270225 - C96 - 148/210/5 - PB - 9781861511935 - Gloss Lamination